Insid

i

OTHER TITLES BY THE SAME AUTHOR

Inside your PC

by

Ian Sinclair

BERNARD BABANI (publishing) LTD
THE GRAMPIANS
SHEPHERDS BUSH ROAD
LONDON W6 7NF
ENGLAND

© 1997 BERNARD BABANI (publishing) LTD

First Published –November 1997

British Library Cataloguing in Publication Data:

A catalogue record for this book is available from the British Library

ISBN 0 85934 438 X

Cover Design by Gregor Arthur
Cover Illustration by Adam Willis
Printed and Bound in Great Britain by Cox & Wyman Ltd., Reading

iv

ABOUT THIS BOOK

For every PC computer user who regards the machine as a tool to be used but never understood, there is another who would like to know what is inside the box, but has been discouraged from trying to find out.

Much of the air of mystery that surrounds computers has been aided by manuals that are not exactly helpful, and this stems from the early days when only enthusiasts bought computers. You don't have to tell enthusiasts more than the bare facts, and that's what so many manuals do. Some computers arrive with only the bare minimum of manuals and nothing that helps you if anything has to be altered.

Another difficulty is that many publishers and wholesale book buyers think that everybody knows everything about computers, and that if they need information, it should be in a £25 book from a US publisher. Both of these assumptions are false, but they have resulted in computer shops stocking American books that either provide only for the expert or which insult the reader even with the title.

This book is intended for anyone, of any age, who uses a computer and wants to have some inkling of how it works. It is a non-technical description of what lies inside the box and what each part does. I don't expect you to read this to become a computer mechanic, but to know at least as much about your computer as you might know about a car, a motorbike, or a washing machine. Apart from anything else, there is a lot of satisfaction to be got from knowing what's inside, and in practical terms, you can make a more informed choice about your next computer or about upgrading your present one. That's all.

Ian Sinclair

Summer 1997

WARNING

Though this book is concerned with what is inside your PC, this should not be taken to mean that children or anyone without experience of electrical equipment should open the box. There is nothing harmful about looking at the inside of a computer, but I must emphasise that this has to be done when the power is unplugged. Children should be supervised if they want to see inside, and on no account should internal parts be touched, either with fingers, metal tools, or anything else.

ABOUT THE AUTHOR

Ian Sinclair was born in 1932 in Tayport, Fife, and graduated from the University of St. Andrews in 1956. In that year, he joined the English Electric Valve Co. in Chelmsford, Essex, to work on the design of specialised cathode-ray tubes, and later on small transmitting valves and TV transmitting tubes.

In 1966, he became an assistant lecturer at Hornchurch Technical College, and in 1967 joined the staff of Braintree College of F.E. as a lecturer. His first book, "Understanding Electronic Components" was published in 1972, and he has been writing ever since, particularly for the novice in Electronics or Computing. The interest in computing arose after seeing a Tandy TRS80 in San Francisco in 1977, and of his 180 published books, about half have been on computing topics, starting with a guide to Microsoft Basic on the TRS80 in 1979.

He left teaching in 1984 to concentrate entirely on writing, and has also gained experience in computer typesetting, particularly for mathematical texts. He has recently visited Seattle to see Microsoft at work, and to remind them that he has been using Microsoft products longer than most Microsoft employees can remember.

ACKNOWLEDGEMENTS

I would like to thank the friendly and helpful staff of Text 100 Ltd. for providing the MS-DOS and Windows 95 software on which this book has been based, and Word 97 on which it was composed and typeset.

I would also like to thank Julie Girone Gwin of the Microsoft Museum for showing me the collection of vintage desktop computers and jogging my recollections of them.

TRADEMARKS

CONTENTS

Preface

To many users of a PC, the inside is a no-go area, wrapped in mystery, and beyond normal human understanding. This view has been encouraged by the use of programs that need no more than the ability to click a mouse button, and for many users, particularly in the older age groups, this suits them very well. If, however, you hate working with something that you do not understand you will find much of interest here.

Younger PC users have no problems about the PC, and one of their most frequent questions is "how does it work?". It's a question that could be answered in a shorter book twenty years ago, but we have come a long way in computing since then.

In fact, the principles on which your PC works have not really changed much since the days when a Commodore PET or a Tandy TRS80 was the last word in technology. What has changed most is the scale of the machine, packing much more into much the same space. It's what has been packed in since the mid 1970s that makes this book rather longer than it would have been in these early days.

For any newcomer to computing, the whole topic seems impossibly complicated, with each new machine becoming out of date in a few months. In addition, advertisements and articles are often in a form of gobbledegook that you feel you cannot learn quickly enough. If you were a newcomer to cars, you might feel the same way, but you don't because you have grown up with cars.

The modern generation will grow up with computers, and will be familiar with all the terms, just as an older generation was with car-speak. This book has been designed particularly for the young reader who is starting along the path to computing, or the older reader who thinks that it is too late to make any effort.

Inside your PC

I need to make one point clear at this stage. You might want to look inside your own computer to see what's there. If you have a desktop type of machine, that's fine as long as you remember electrical safety — switch off and take the plug out. Do not attempt to look inside a portable, laptop, or other type of miniature computer, because the arrangement of the parts is very different though it works in the same way. Desktop (and tower-case) machines are all very similar internally, and that makes it easier to describe where the various bits are as well as what they do.

Your age is not important, but your interest is. The ability to understand how a computer works does not need great intellect or a scientific background, just curiosity, interest, imagination and some patience. These are qualities that do not depend on age. The most difficult part of it all is to explain how simple the machine really is, because users expect it to be complicated. A brick is simple, but if you can take in the idea of a brick, you can take in the idea of a house built from bricks. The computer is made from very simple units, and it's the number of these units and their arrangement that makes it all appear so complicated.

If all that whets your appetite, well and good. In this book, we start from scratch, assuming nothing. It's better that way, because if you know too much you are likely to expect complications that are not here. Whether you are nine or ninety, this can provide you with the knowledge that allows you to hold your own with the computer buffs, with the advantage that you can explain it all in clear English.

1 Opening the box

Let's open the box, the main box. You don't need to open up your own computer unless you want to, but at some stage you will probably want to take a look. Just remember electrical safety — switch off at the mains and take the plug out of the socket before you open the case. If your computer is a portable type forget about opening it, and just read on, because portable computers are not designed for opening, only for using. **At this point, please read the warning on page vii — children cannot be expected to know about electrical safety nor about the damage that can be caused by touching electronics circuits.**

Some boxes are hinged, and you open the lid by pressing in two buttons and lifting. Others have a sliding case, and you have to unscrew or unclip a fastener and pull the cover away from a steel frame. Now what do you see inside?

Yes, there are certainly a lot of wires and connectors. There are also circuit boards. These are the flat brown sheets that are covered with black slabs. The slabs are the silicon chips that you hear so much about, and the boards are there to support the chips and to make electrical connections between them.

Any metal can be used to make electrical connections, and the metal on the boards is thin copper strip, often silver-coated. It is put there by a combination of photography and printing, and that's why the board is called a printed circuit board, or PCB. You will see the printed connections on one side of the board, and there are more on the other side. You will have to take my word for it that there are more of them between the sides that you cannot see. The circuit boards on your computer hold and connect the essential chips that make it work the way it does.

Inside your PC

The power supply

Whatever type of computer you open up, there will be a sealed metal box, with some ventilation holes, inside. This metal box contains the power supply, and it has a fan built into one end to help keep the computer cool.

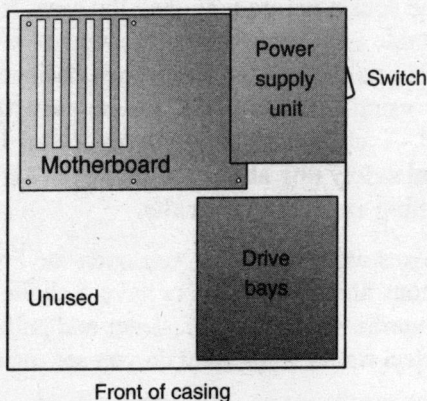

Front of casing

Figure 1. Looking inside at the power supply

Computers use low voltage electrical supplies. How low? Typical voltages are 3.3, 5, and 12 volts — all too low to give you an electric shock. These voltages are steady, the type we call DC, meaning direct current, the type you could get from batteries. The trouble is that large computers would drain batteries very quickly, so they take their electrical supply from the house mains.

Nothing is ever that easy. The house mains supply uses a high voltage, around 230 volts, and it's also a different type, called AC. AC means alternating current, and what it amounts to is that the voltage rises and falls 50 times a second. If you could see electricity, AC would look like a wave. There are three good reasons for this. One is that it's easy to generate, another is that it's easy to take from one

4

place to another. The third is that it's easy to convert one AC voltage into another.

That's what the power supply box does. Outside the box, all the wires and copper strips work with low voltage, with no risk of shock. Inside the box, the high voltage AC supply is converted into these low voltage supplies. The box encloses all the dangerous parts, and everything outside it is safe.

Safe doesn't mean that you should touch anything. Your skin is always moist, and if you grab a printed circuit board carelessly you can leave a sweaty mark that will carry electricity from one copper strip to another. This might cause no problems, but in some parts of a board it could stop the computer from working correctly. Unless you know exactly where touching is harmless, don't do it.

- **You must not, on any account try to open the monitor, a printer, or any other attachments to the computer. These items contain points that can be at very high voltages, and should be opened only by an experienced engineer.**

The power supply, then, doesn't do any computing action; it only provides power for the smarter bits. Portable computers can use batteries, but batteries do not provide power for very long, so that some type of mains power supply is needed also. The power supply on a portable computer will usually recharge the batteries as well.

The motherboard

When you open the box, the largest board that you see is the one that is called the **motherboard**. It gets that name because it carries all the other boards plugged into it, and it contains all the main chips and connections for the computing actions. You can update your computer by replacing the motherboard — it's like putting a new engine into a car.

Inside your PC

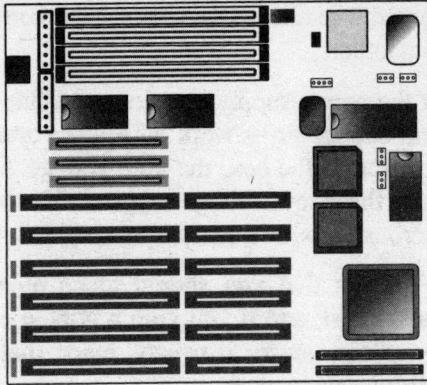

Figure 2. A typical motherboard

Most computers use a set of standardised fastening points for the motherboard, so that you can take an old motherboard out and put a new one in. There are, however, exceptions, and most of them are the 'famous name' computers. If your computer is a 'Brand X' type, assembled from standard parts by a firm you never heard of, it will probably be easy and cheap to upgrade with standard parts. It's all part of Sinclair's Law of Shopping, the less you pay the more you get for your money.

Drives

The part of your computer that looks like a multi-storey car park (either upright or on its side) is the set of disc drives. A computer disc (sometimes spelled **disk**) stores information just as a compact disc stores music, and your computer needs to be able to work with more than one type of disc. The disc players of the computer are called drives, and modern computers have three. One is for small amounts of information, and is called the floppy drive. One is for large amounts of information and is the hard drive. The third is for information on compact discs and is called the CD-ROM drive. You can put small discs into and out of the floppy drive and you can put CDs into and out of the CD-ROM drive, but the hard drive is fixed — it stays inside the computer.

Cables and connectors

There are bundles of cables and connectors inside your computer. Many of these come from the power supply, taking the electrical supply to the motherboard and to each disc drive. Others are used to carry information, and these cables are often ribbon cables. They consist of a set of wires laid side by side, and each cable looks like a ribbon. One wire is usually coloured or striped to show you which way round the cable is fitted. A connector is fitted at each end of these data cables. These connectors grip the cable and have metal teeth that pierce into the wires of the cable to make contact. Careless handling can break one or more connections, causing the computer to stop working.

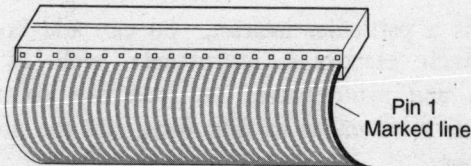

Pin 1
Marked line

Figure 3. A typical data cable and its connector

Expansion slots

The motherboard contains a line of sockets, near the back of the case. Some of these will have a circuit board plugged into them, others will be unused. These are the expansion slots of your computer. Their purpose is to adapt your computer for other actions. If you want to use your computer as an editor for video tapes you plug in a board for video editing. If you want to use your computer to read pages from a book you plug in a board for a gadget called a scanner. When anything new comes along, all you need to do is plug in the board — you don't normally need to buy a new computer.

Some boards are already plugged in. One is usually for controlling the picture display. Old PC models could display only words, and a board, called a graphics board, was needed if you wanted to see pictures. Nowadays, this board is already in place, but if you want to add to its actions (like being able to display video pictures) you can replace the old board with a newer one.

Another board that is usually fitted into a slot when you buy the computer is the sound board. As the name tells you, this connects the computer to loudspeakers so that you can have sound effects and music. The sound board is particularly needed if you want to use multimedia, meaning combinations of words, pictures, and sound from a CD. With a sound board you can also send sound signals into the computer, so that you can record your voice and even have your spoken words appear as printed words on the screen.

If music is a particular interest, you can add boards that connect with electronic instruments such as guitars, keyboards and synthesisers, and you can control these instruments, store music as disc files, edit the music, and other actions.

In fact, it's not too much to claim that the PC computer can be useful to you no matter what your interests are. With all that going for it, why not learn more about what's inside?

2 Bits and bytes

Computers are sometimes called 'number-crunchers'. That's because all they can really do is work on numbers. Perhaps you thought that working with numbers just means adding and subtracting, multiplying and dividing? In fact, there are many more actions that you can do with numbers, and what makes the computer special is that it can work fast. It can't think, but it can do what it's told to do pretty quickly.

ASCII and other codes

If a computer can deal only with numbers, how does it work with words? It's easier than you think — each character, meaning letter of the alphabet, each digit from 0 to 9, and each symbol like commas and full stops is coded as a number. Of course, this can work only if all computers use the same number codes. These codes represent your data, the information that you want the computer to work with.

The code that all computers use is called ASCII. This is the first letters of the name American Standard Code for Information Interchange, so we can be glad they shortened it. The ASCII code uses numbers 32 to 127 for letters, digits, and symbols. Now that computers are utilised world-wide, the numbers 128 to 255 are also used so that letters and symbols that are not in the English language can be coded. The full set of codes from 32 to 255 is called extended ASCII or ANSI.

How do we code a picture? There are two methods. One is to think of a picture as a set of dots arranged in rows and columns, and give each dot a number, like the number of a house in a street. For each dot, another number is used to code how bright the dot is and what its colour is. In this way you can code a picture as a set of numbers. This way of coding a picture is like printing a map, and it's called **bit-mapping**. There are several ways of bit-mapping a picture, so computers have to be able to work with any of them.

Inside your PC

The other way to code a picture is as a set of lines. For each line, you can use numbers to show the position of the start and the end of the line, and you can also use numbers to code the shape of the line. This type of coding is called a **vector** code, and once again there are several varieties of code.

What about sounds? Long before computers were around we knew that a sound was caused by vibration, and we could measure the pitch of sound (meaning high notes or low notes). This pitch is the number of vibrations in each second, so it's not difficult to code sound into numbers. The difficulty is that sounds change quickly — music doesn't consist of just one note. That in turn means that we have to use a lot of numbers for a short piece of music. Sound that has been converted into numbers like this is digital sound and it's recorded in this way onto compact discs.

Two by two

The numbers that we normally use have come about because we have ten fingers, so we count from 0 to 9, and then the next number is coded as 10, meaning 1 ten and no units. The number we write as 156 is one hundred, five tens and six units. A hundred is ten tens, and a thousand is ten hundreds, so that number scale goes up by ten times for each column we use for writing the number.

Electrical circuits cannot cope easily with tens and the most reliable action that we know is switching on and off. If we use the digit 0 to mean off and 1 to mean on, this allows us to count with these two digits. This type of number scale is called a binary scale.

How do we count with just two digits? Just the same way as we do with ten. Counting up, we start with 0, and then 1. There isn't any other digit, and the next number is 10, meaning a two and no units. Following that is 11, meaning a two and a unit (totalling 3). What comes next?

Yes, 100, meaning a four, no twos and no units, and that is followed by 101, one four, no twos and a unit (totalling 5). Any number that we can use in the scale of ten we can convert to a scale of two — we don't need to worry about how it is done at the moment.

The important point is that electrical switches can carry out any kind of number crunching if the numbers are in this scale of two, called a binary scale. Digitising means converting a quantity into these binary numbers, and a digital device is one that uses these numbers. The number crunching need not just be arithmetic, either. One very important use of scale of two is to express logic.

Logic means how we find an answer to a question, and computers would never have been possible if a man called George Boole had not discovered that all the rules of logic could be written in terms of scale of two. This was in 1854, long before computers were thought of, at a time when railways were such a novelty that people tried to stop them from being built.

Boole found that all logic processes could be expressed by using three simple actions called AND, OR and NOT. AND means that two conditions must both be true. If you say, *I'll go to the cinema if George goes and Emma goes* you are using the AND logic. You mean that if either George or Emma drops out, you won't go. The OR action is that either one of two conditions must be true. If you say, *I'll go to the cinema if George or Emma goes,* you mean that you will go with George or with Emma or with both of them. The NOT action is simpler, and you might *say I'll go to the cinema if George doesn't go* — that's a NOT action.

Boole showed that AND, OR and NOT rules could be written in binary form. We needn't go into detail, but because the rules could be written in binary they could be carried out using electric currents and switches. At a time when Charles Babbage was trying to build a mechanical computer using gearwheels, and electricity was not well understood, this was advanced thinking. The first use of Boole's logic with switches was in railway signalling.

Bytes

The digits 0 and 1 that are used in a binary scale are binary digits, and we shorten this to **bits**. The early computers often used numbers that consisted of eight bits, and this group of eight became known as a **byte**. Even today, when computers work with 32 or 64 bits at a time, we still use the byte as our unit for size, particularly for memory (see later). These bits are data, the numbers that the computer crunches.

Crunching

What about this number-crunching? What does the computer do when we press the 'A' key and see the shape of the letter 'A' on the screen?

It's simple enough. When you press the key, it closes a switch, and that switch operates a circuit that creates the code for that key. All of that work is done inside the keyboard, and the code is sent to the computer.

Key   Main computer   Graphics board   Monitor

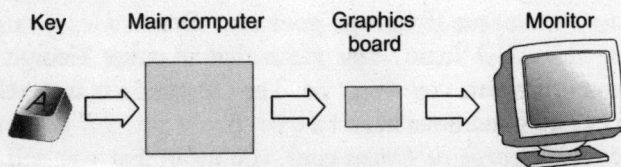

Figure 4. Passing a code from key to monitor

The computer receives the code and all it does is pass it on to the board that controls the display, the graphics board. This board uses the number code to control circuits that create TV signals, and these signals display the letter on the screen. All the computer has done with the number code is to pass it to the right place, and that's what a lot of number-crunching is.

How about more advanced number crunching? Suppose that when you pressed the 'A' key you wanted the screen to display 'a', the small (lower-case) letter? The keyboard and the graphics board actions are much the same, but the computer takes the ASCII code from the keyboard and adds the number 32. That's because the ASCII code has been designed that way — the code for the small letter is 32 more than the code for the capital letter.

All the actions that are possible depend on shifting or altering codes like these simple examples. You can shift codes from the keyboard to a printer so that the computer works like a typewriter. You can alter picture codes, changing colours and positions of parts of the picture, and then shift the codes to a printer to print the picture on paper. You can alter codes on sound, changing its pitch or speed of playing so that it sounds different when you shift the codes to the sound board and hear them from the loudspeaker.

All of this means that the computer actions are not always the same. Codes might be shifted one way or another, numbers might be added or taken away, even multiplied or divided. This is something we don't often have to think about normally. When we switch on a light in the house, the same switch always works the same light. The same CD always plays the same music.

What makes the computer different is that the result of an action need not be the same each time. The circuits inside your computer can be used like a telephone exchange, making different connections. These connections are controlled by codes, and this action is called programming. For example, we could arrange the programming so that when we sent the code 0 the circuits were connected one way, and when we sent the code 1 the circuits were connected another way.

13

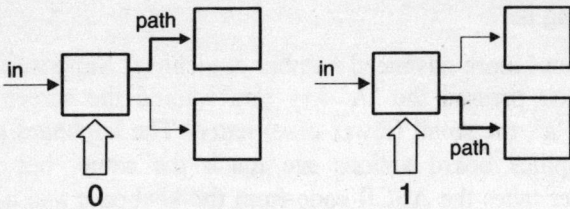

Figure 5. Switching connections

The programmable chip

A telephone exchange is a simple example of programming. Your telephone can carry both the programming signals (dialling numbers) and information (your voice). You pick up the phone and you program it by dialling a number. This connects you to somebody else and you talk (they say it's good to talk). Another time, when you pick up the phone you might not talk with the same person, so you dial a different number. This programs the exchange to connect you so you can talk with this other person. Both the dialling codes and your voice signals share the same lines, and the difference is that you have to send the dialling codes first and the voice signals later.

Computers became possible when we discovered faster ways of dealing with codes, but the way that codes are used has not changed. Nowadays, the switching actions are done by a silicon chip, one of the black slabs on the motherboard. Send this chip one code and it will add numbers, send it another code and it will multiply numbers. The numbers that it has to work on are sent following the program code. Suppose that the number 115 meant 'add', and you wanted to add 12 and 17. You would send the codes 115 12 17 to the chip, and the signal that came out would be 29, the result of adding 12 to 17. You might use the code 140 to mean sending a number to the graphics board, so that the codes 140 65 would print the letter 'A' on the screen — 65 is the ASCII code for 'A'.

Even more important is the use of AND, OR and NOT. Because these actions compare binary numbers, they also can be carried out by the microprocessor. We can send a code meaning AND, followed by the two numbers that are being compared in this way, and get the answer out.

Making connections in silicon

Computers are very new if you are old, but if you are young you might think they have been about for ever. The first computers were mechanical, and they were programmed by changing gearwheels. Later, they were programmed by changing connections between metal pins, rather like a miniature telephone exchange. Nowadays there is nothing that we can see because all the connections are made or broken inside a block of solid material called silicon.

Silicon (not silicone, please) is peculiar. Most materials will either carry electric current or not, they are either conductors or insulators. Silicon is neither, and tiny amounts of material added to it will change it from being an insulator into being a conductor. It's a semiconductor, and what makes is even more peculiar is that we can make a tiny piece of silicon into an electrical switch by adding different materials to different parts.

This switching action uses three connections to the silicon. One is the controller, called a gate. When there is no connection to the gate, no electric current can flow between the other two connections. When there is a voltage at the gate, the other two connections conduct just as if there was a piece of wire between them. The whole unit is an electrically controlled switch. It's called a metal-oxide-semiconductor field effect transistor, and to save wear on your tongue we shorten it to MOSFET.

What makes modern computers possible is the incredibly small size that we can achieve for a MOSFET, so that millions of them can be placed on a thin wafer of silicon the size of your thumbnail. Not only can we make the MOSFETs in this small size, but we can also make connections between them so that one switch can control another or several others. A wafer of silicon that has been created with these connections is called an IC, meaning integrated circuit, and it's what we mean by a silicon chip.

Silicon chips were invented in the 1950s, and they were intended to make electrical equipment more reliable. The more connections you make with wire, the less reliable is your electrical equipment, and using a silicon chip meant that much less wire was used. More reliable equipment was needed for the space rockets, so that silicon chips were in great demand, and the more they could replace wires the better. Manufacturers set out to make chips that contained more and more MOSFETs and connections, and that's where the modern computer chips came from.

The black slab that you see on the motherboard and on plug-in boards is just a holder for the chip. This protects the chip against moisture and vibration, and allows connections to be made through sturdy pins rather than through thin wires.

The microprocessor

The microprocessor is the most important chip in a computer because it carries out most of the computing actions. On the motherboard of a modern computer it is the large square block with (about) 248 connectors.

What does it do? The answer is almost everything that you can do with numbers. It can add, subtract, multiply, and divide. It can compare numbers and decide if they are equal or if one is larger. It can use logic actions such as AND, OR and NOT. That is about all that is needed, and the cleverness lies in making it all happen very fast and in a small space.

A microprocessor needs a large number of connections. Modern microprocessors work with 32 bits of data at a time, and there has to be a connector for each bit. In addition, the microprocessor must be able to make connections to other chips by using a number (an address), and this needs 32 bits, another 32 connections. There are also large numbers of connections needed for controlling other chips, and for DC power supplies. This is why so many microprocessor chips are mounted into a casing that has 248 or more pins.

How it started

The microprocessor started as a military project in the USA, intended to be a logic circuit that could be programmed. The project was cancelled, leaving the manufacturer, Intel, with a large number of chips that had no obvious uses. Just at that time, however, a group of students were interested in using such chips for a simple computer, and they found that the Intel chip was ideal. Very soon, a small firm called Altair was making and selling computer kits all over the USA and Intel realised that their chip could be used for small computers.

These first machines were very simple. Several hours of work on programming could just about make the machine flash lights on and off in a pattern, but not much more was possible.

That was the start, however, and more capable chips followed, with small computers being built with keyboards and monitors, the sort of machine that we would recognise as a computer today. They still had to be programmed by the user, but very soon it became possible to buy ready-made programs on cassette tape.

We can date this to around 1978, so that you can see that there have been huge changes to the present day. Today's computers are vastly more capable and easier to use, but they lack the fascination and the joy of discovery that the old ones had. I count myself lucky for having been around then.

Inside your PC

The microcode

Every microprocessor that we use in a PC uses the same system. You feed in a number that represents a program instruction, and follow it with one or more numbers that it has to work on. It's the instruction we want to look at for the moment.

A single number may not be enough to code all the switching actions that set up the microprocessor to carry out an action, so that the programming number itself is just a code. Inside the microprocessor, the programming number is checked to find if it is valid — using a number that was incorrect might cause the whole machine to stop. Once the code has been checked, it is used to locate a whole set of codes. These are the codes that are then used for programming. We call these **microcodes**.

There are several reasons for this. One is that the microprocessor stores a microcode for each valid instruction. This ensures that no other instructions can be carried out. It also guards against incorrect instructions causing conflicting settings (like trying to switch on and off at the same time). It avoids the need to use large numbers as instruction codes. It also allows the manufacturers to upgrade their chips by using more efficient microcode for the same instruction.

Connections and buses.

The microprocessor sits, like a spider in its web, at the heart of the computer. It must make connections with all the other parts of the machine, such as the drives and the memory. Now you might think that the best way to do this would be to make a set of connections to each drive and a set to the memory, but that's not easy. If you wanted to send 32 bits to the floppy drive, 32 to the hard drive, read 32 from the CD ROM and send 32 to the memory you would need 128 connecting lines, all of them connected to the microprocessor. Though it's not impossible, it's not easy.

18

What is done, then, is to use a bus. It's not a double-decker; the word comes from *omnibus* (Latin), meaning for all. The 32 pins for data are connected to a set of 32 metal lines, and everything else plugs into the same 32 lines. They really are for all. Fig. 6 shows a diagram that is used for training service engineers — it shows how the buses, represented by broad lines, link each part of the computer. You don't need to know what each part does, only that they are linked by the buses.

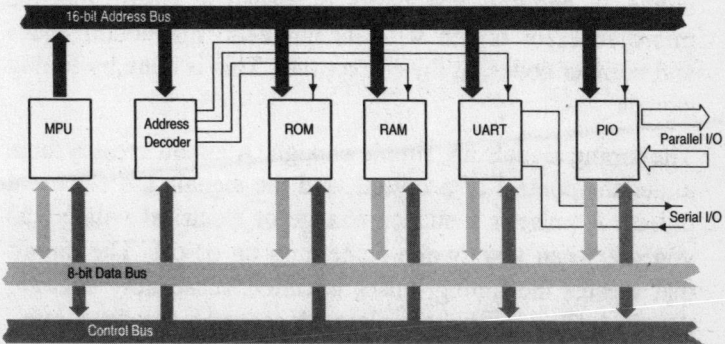

Figure 6. A Bus diagram

The use of a bus is a simple way of making sure that every part of the computer can be connected to the data signals, but how do we make sure that the signals reach the right parts? If we send out a number from the microprocessor, how can we make it affect the hard drive rather than one of the other units?

The answer is to use control signals. For each device there are one or two connections for control signals. One connection is used for the signal that this is the device that is to be connected, the other signals whether the device is reading or writing, receiving data or sending it. All other devices will receive control signals that disconnect them from the data bus.

♦ As the diagram shows, more than one bus is used, and the usual score is one data bus, one address bus and one control bus. Like all buses, you wait for one and three turn up.

Timing

The last piece in the jigsaw is timing. If all the units share the data bus, they can't all be active at the same time, and there has to be some way of deciding when each one is active. In addition, some way is needed to ensure that the microprocessor is fed with its numbers, instruction codes and number codes, at the correct rate. This is done by timing signals.

The timing signals are simple enough. A circuit creates them under the control of a crystal, and the signals are electrical pulses. A pulse is a sudden change of electrical voltage, as you get when you switch something on or off. The circuit that creates the timing pulses is called, reasonably enough, the clock. The number of pulses per second is the clock rate.

Now you may be used to clocks and watches that move a hand each second, but a rate of one pulse per second would certainly not be fast enough for a computer. We measure clock rates in units called megahertz (abbreviated to MHz), meaning millions of pulses per second.

That might sound fast, but in computing terms it's not. The early computers used clock rates of 2 MHz or so, and with advanced design some could use as much as 4 MHz. The first PC machines used 8 MHz, and steady improvement over the years has resulted in chips that can work with clock speeds that would have been thought quite impossible only a few years ago. At the time of writing, fast computers are using 233 MHz, and it's possible that we shall have 400 MHz quite soon.

This clock rate affects the speed of the machine, though it's not the only factor. It does affect how 'modern' a machine is, however, and computers that run at 75 MHz are now thought of as ancient, though they were once the fastest thing on microcodes.

3 Memory

Why does a computer need memory? The answer is that it's the only satisfactory way of feeding the microprocessor with bytes. If the microprocessor needs to read a new byte ten million times per second, you certainly can't type at that speed. The codes are placed in the memory and the microprocessor helps itself, reading the memory each time it needs some data.

What is this memory? Nothing that you will find particularly new. A unit of memory is just a switch that connects with either a 0 or a 1 signal. Eight units make up a byte of memory, and what we need to understand is how the microprocessor can make use of these memory units.

As it happens, one byte is a very small amount of memory. In the early days, we used units called kilobytes (Kbyte), each Kbyte being 1024 bytes. Nowadays, even the Kbyte is too small a unit, and memory is measured in megabytes (Mbyte), with 1 Mbyte = 1024 Kbyte. I am using a computer with 32 Mbyte of memory, and by next year I shall probably need 64 Mbyte.

Why 1024? It's a power of two, two multiplied by itself ten times. If you want to write it out, it is:

$2 \times 2 \times 2 \times 2 \times 2 \times 2 \times 2 \times 2 \times 2 \times 2$ (count them, all ten)

and it's the nearest power of two to 1000.

Addressing

You'll remember that the microprocessor needs to be supplied with bytes, the number codes, in a strict sequence. Each instruction code must be followed by the number codes it works on. In addition, the microprocessor must be able to pick out items that might not be in any sequence. The microprocessor must be able to read the memory, meaning that the byte in the memory unit is copied to the microprocessor. It must also be able to write to the memory, meaning that the byte sent out by the microprocessor is stored into the memory.

♦ This means that the memory is changed only when we write to it, not when we read from it.

The use of memory is controlled by address numbers. Now there is nothing complicated about this. Your postman uses this system to find a house in a town street, so this letter goes to number 7 and that letter to number 12, and so on. The microprocessor can locate any unit of memory by generating an address number. On a modern machine, this is a 32-bit binary number.

There are connections (32 of them) for these address numbers, and they are connected as an address **bus**, meaning that all the parts of the computer that use the addressing system are connected to the bus. When the microprocessor places an address code on the bus and signals that the memory is enabled for reading, the address number locates the correct bytes in the memory. The control signals for reading and enabling then ensure that the bytes in the memory are copied to the data bus.

Volatility

We need some memory that is volatile and some that is not. Most memory is **volatile**; meaning that when the computer is switched off the memory loses all stored information. When you switch on again, each memory cell might start up with a 0 or a 1, at random, so the computer clears all the memory to make a fresh start.

There's a snag, though. A microprocessor with no program is useless, like record player with no records. There has to be some memory that keeps its data even while the computer is off. This data will never change, so the memory can consist of permanent connections. We call it ROM, meaning read-only memory.

The ROM need not be large, but it must contain the correct codes in the correct sequence to allow the computer to respond to the keyboard and to operate the hard drive and the floppy drive. This allows it to read in more instructions which can be stored in volatile memory while the computer is switched on. If this ROM is not present the computer cannot work.

The volatile memory can be used to hold the main program bytes and data bytes. It does not matter that the data will be lost when you switch off the computer because it will be read from the hard drive again when you switch on again. What you must remember, however, is that if you generate any data, like typing a letter, it must be saved to the hard drive (or a floppy) to make sure that you can use it again. What you don't save, you can't get back.

Another advantage of using just a small amount of code in the ROM is that it allows you to improve the performance of your computer easily. The ROM contains just enough code to allow the machine to read in more code from a drive. If you change the code that is read in, you can improve performance, and this is much easier than changing the ROM chip or the whole computer. This code in ROM is sometimes called 'bootstrap code'. The name comes from the old fantasy that you could lift yourself into the air by pulling on your own bootstraps.

RAM memory

Most of the memory that is contained in the computer is volatile, and we call it RAM. The name means random-access memory, and though a better name would be read/write memory, the old name has stuck. The reason for the old name is that memory was once made in a form that stored bytes in order, and the only way to get to the 40th byte was to read out the 39 that came before it. Modern memory can be read by sending out an address number and using the data number that comes along the data lines.

At one time, static memory was used for the main memory. A unit of static memory consists of a pair of switches, one on, and the other off. With one switch of a pair on, this represents 1, and the other way round it represents 0. This type of memory can be read and written very quickly, but because one of the two switches is always on, it takes a lot of electric current if the memory is of a reasonable size. Static memory is very expensive, hundreds of pounds for 256 Kbyte, so that using static memory for 32 Mbyte or so would make your computer very fast, but not a bargain offer.

The solution is to use a design for memory that is less power consuming and cheaper to make. This type is called **dynamic** RAM, and what is dynamic about it is that it forgets quickly and has to be reminded. The only way that we can store electricity is a device called a capacitor, and we can make miniature versions using silicon, inside a chip, and with all the connections also on the chip. So far, so good.

Refreshing memory

You use a capacitor to store electricity (electric charge), so that a charged capacitor represents 1 and an uncharged capacitor represents 0. Now for the size of capacitor that we can make on silicon, the charge will leak away in about a thousandth of a second. That's not long by human standards, but the microprocessor is, typically, working with 150 million clock pulse in each second. A time of a thousandth of a second is the time of 150,000 of these clock pulses, which is quite a long time by microprocessor standards.

What makes the use of dynamic memory possible is refreshing. This means that every thousandth of a second, each cell that stores a 1 is re-charged. This is done automatically, and it ensures that the memory contents are maintained for as long as the refreshing continues, which is as long as the power is switched on.

This refreshing action was once a problem that made it impossible to use dynamic memory with fast microprocessors, but clever design has improved things by using memory in banks, see later.

Speed of memory

The speed of memory means the time that it takes between putting an address on the address bus and reading or writing the unit of memory. You have probably guessed by now that it's a short time. Computing nowadays deals with some very big amounts, like Mbytes, and some very small ones. The unit that we use for timing around the microprocessor is the nanosecond (ns), and one ns is one thousandth of a millionth of a second. Written as a fraction this is 1/1,000,000,000 second, and you will also see it written as 10^{-9} seconds (9 is the number of zeros).

An average dynamic RAM chip will have a speed of around 70 ns, so that it places data on the data bus 70 ns after its address appears on the address bus. That sounds good, but remember that the time between microprocessor clock pulses is around six ns. This makes it all look impossible, but there are ways of getting around it, which amount to sending out the address well before you need to send or receive data.

Incidentally, static RAM can achieve 6 ns times fairly easily, so that it can be used to store data, reading from the slower dynamic RAM when it has a chance, and feeding the microprocessor when data is needed. This type of action is called caching, meaning hiding, and this type of memory is called fast cache memory. We'll come back to that point.

Memory banking

Memory banks are groups of memory cells, and the cleverness consists in refreshing one bank of memory while the microprocessor is using another bank. Another advantage of this bank system is that the speed of the memory need not be as great as the speed of the microprocessor.

All modern computers arrange memory in banks, and you will find as a result that when you want to upgrade a computer you cannot add just one bank of chips, you must add in pairs.

4 Instructions

Instruction codes are the key to the way that your computer works. The microprocessor and the other chips and gadgets are all very clever, but without program instructions they are totally useless. We have to take a deep breath now and see what the sequence of actions is for an instruction.

This means knowing what happens inside the microprocessor. We don't need to know in detail, but the important point is that the microprocessor consists of a large number of circuits called registers. These registers are created from switch units and they can carry out a set of actions:

- they can be loaded with bits,
- they can store bits,
- they can carry out arithmetic and logic actions on bits,
- they can feed out bits either one by one or in groups.

One very important register is the address counter register, often called the instruction pointer (IP). This register contains the address number (memory address) for the next instruction that the microprocessor will want to use. When the microprocessor has completed an instruction, it can read the next program code from the address that is held in the IP. How does it do this? Easy, its internal switches (controlled by microcode) connect the IP register to the address bus pins.

Use of memory and processor

Each instruction is dealt with by what is called a fetch–execute cycle, and each cycle is simple. It's the number and speed that makes the computer a smart device. Lets look at a typical cycle that uses an instruction and two bytes of data that are to be added.

The cycle starts with the microprocessor reading an instruction. The instruction (in this example, the add instruction) will have been read from the memory location whose address number is stored in the IP register. Immediately this number has been used it will be incremented — meaning that it is increased by one unit. This action prepares for reading the next byte.

The instruction is read along the data lines into a special register. The number is compared with all the numbers used to locate microcodes, and when a match is found, the microcode instructions will be acted on. If no match is found, the microprocessor will run a special program that stops the computer and prints an error message.

The microcode sets the microprocessor to read the first part of the data. This is usually read into a register called the **Accumulator**, though other registers can be used. The IP is incremented again, and the second byte is read into a register that serves the Add unit. At the same time, the accumulator is connected to the second input of the Add unit. At the next clock pulse, the connections change, and the result of the addition is read from the add unit back to the accumulator. What happens then depends on how the program is arranged, and the usual action is to store the result somewhere in the memory.

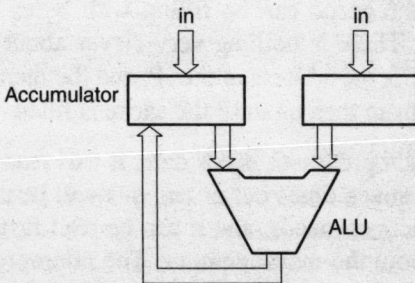

Figure 7. Using the ALU, accumulator and another register to add numbers

Inside your PC

What we have called the Add unit is in fact capable of much more, and its correct name is the Arithmetic and Logic unit, ALU. The ALU has two inputs and an output and its internal connections can be arranged to carry out whatever arithmetic or logical action the microcode specifies. What all have in common is that one byte is always taken from the accumulator, and the answer is always returned to the accumulator, as the diagram shows.

It's a simple enough action, but it takes several clock pulses, even in this example where we have assumed that the numbers are just single-byte numbers. We have ignored complications like numbers of many bytes, what happens when an addition produces a carry, and so on. The important point is that the microprocessor breaks down each main action into a set of small steps, and carries out each step quickly. Some simple actions may need only one clock pulse; others can take several hundred.

Purpose of a cache

A cache is a piece of fast memory, and its purpose is to feed the microprocessor with data in advance. This allows the microprocessor to work faster than it could if it used the main memory. While the microprocessor is working on an instruction, the cache can be filling with bytes taken from the memory. There is nothing very clever about this — the starting point is the address in the IP, and the memory is read in sequence from then on until the cache is filled.

When the microprocessor needs data, it will read it from the cache. Some seven times out of ten, this will be the data that the microprocessor needs, and it can be read faster from the cache than from the main memory. The microprocessor can check that the data from the cache is correct by comparing the address numbers.

What happens if the cache does not contain the correct data? The microprocessor will then have to rely on reading memory instead, filling the cache from a new address. This refill might take longer than a normal read from memory. If you can be very fast seven times and slightly slow three times, you are still working faster than you would if you had to make each read action from slow memory.

Some microprocessor chips have a cache built into the chip, and all can make use of a cache consisting of fast memory on the motherboard. The way that the cache is used can have a large effect on the speed of a computer, much more than just increasing the clock rate.

Interrupts

From what you have read so far, you might think that the microprocessor starts reading from the first address in the memory and carries on until there is nothing more to do. It doesn't, and one of the many exceptions is when the processor is repeating a few instructions over and over again. This is called a loop, and it's a way of waiting for some action, like your response to the message *Press any key*. Another exception is a jump when the microprocessor will use either one piece of code or another.

Another thing that can affect the progress of a set of instructions is called an **interrupt**. It's very important, but like so many other actions is not difficult to understand.

What do you do when you are interrupted in the middle of a job? The most likely actions are that you set aside what you are doing. Perhaps you might want to scribble a rough note to remind yourself of what you were doing. You then attend to what has interrupted you (put the cat out, answer the doorbell). Once the interruption has been dealt with, you get back, remind yourself what you were doing, and carry on.

The microprocessor handles interrupts in the same way. The interrupt starts when an interrupt signal is received. This is a signal to a pin on the microprocessor, and how that signal is generated is up to the circuit designer. Another path to an

31

interrupt is an instruction that causes an interrupt. A typical source of an interrupt signal is the keyboard, with the interrupt meaning that a key has been pressed.

When the interrupt is received, the microprocessor finishes the instruction it is working on, — it's a case of *I've started so I'll finish*. It then stores the numbers in all of its registers, using a part of the memory that is reserved for this action and called the stack. The next step is to call up a set of instructions for dealing with the interrupt.

These instructions, called the interrupt service routine, are stored in the memory and their address is passed to the microprocessor at the same time as the interrupt signal. The instructions deal with the cause of the interrupt. In this example, they read the keyboard and pass the byte that they read to the memory.

When the interrupt service routine is completed, the microprocessor reads back its register contents from the stack. When the address in the IP has been read and the stack is empty, the microprocessor will start on the instruction that it would have worked on if there had been no interrupt.

Ports

So far, we've concentrated on the microprocessor; as if a load of number crunching was all the computer ever got up to. Now we have to look at how bytes of data get into the microprocessor and how some of them get out again. The answer is by way of ports.

Your ordinary everyday port, air or sea, sends goods out and takes them in from any place that it serves, and the port of a computer does the same. The computer ports are chips on the motherboard, and if you haven't enough you can add more by way of expansion boards.

There are two main types of ports, **serial** and **parallel**. A serial port sends bits out or takes them in one by one, at a slow rate (up to 28,800 bits per second, typically). The port will accept a byte from the microprocessor, and will send its bits out at this slower rate. It can also accept bits in from other devices and assemble them into sets of eight to send to the microprocessor.

The advantage of a serial port is that the signals need only a few wires, as few as two. The cables can be long, up to 100 metres. A few printers can use a serial port, but the most important serial port device is the modem which connects your computer to the Internet. Most computers have two serial ports fitted.

The other type is a parallel port. As the name suggests, this can work with one complete byte of eight bits at a time, and it can pass bytes in and out much faster than a serial port, typically at a rate of 4 MHz or more. The drawback of a parallel port is that the cables need to have at least eight wires, and unless a booster amplifier is used, they need to be less than two metres long.

♦ A parallel port is fitted to your computer so that the printer can be connected, and there are other devices that can be connected to the computer in this way.

What happens at the ports depends on the programming. When data has to be read in or written out, the instructions to the microprocessor will set up the port and start delivering or reading the bytes. Each port chip has a temporary store so that a byte can be held until it is transmitted or completely received, so that the microprocessor does not deal in part-bytes.

How does the microprocessor identify the port? The port is connected to the buses, and when its address is selected with the port enabled, it becomes active. Control signals then determine whether it is reading in or writing out

Inside your PC

The monitor output

The monitor that looks so much like a TV receiver is rather more complicated. To start with it has to be much better than a TV receiver is, as far as picture quality is concerned. That's why a 21 inch monitor costs three times as much as a 21 inch TV.

- **You must never attempt to open a monitor, because it used dangerously high voltages at point that can be touched**.

The monitor uses a screen display, and for a desktop PC the display uses a cathode-ray tube (CRT). Some day, no doubt, there will be flat screens that are bright, light and which don't cost the earth, but they haven't happened yet. Until then we still use the cathode ray tube that has been around for most of the 20th century.

We needn't look at details of how the CRT works, because, after all, it's not inside your computer. The picture that you see is built up by lighting up dots that glow in different colours. The dots are arranged in set of three, and three colours are used, red, green, and blue. These are the three colours of light that make up white light, and by making these dots glow with different amounts of brightness we can create any colour.

These colours, red, green, and blue, are the primary colours of light. If you are mixing paints, you use a different set of colours. That's because paints reflect light, they don't shine with a light of their own.

The picture is created by switching on the dots of light, one at a time. It's a process called scanning, and it's fast, like almost everything else in computing. A modern monitor will scan every set of dots on the screen 85 times in every second. Though the dots are being lit for only a fraction of a second, your eye sees a picture because your eye stores an image for about $^1/_{10}$ of a second. That's what makes cinema and TV possible.

On a colour monitor there are three scanning actions, one for each colour of dot. The monitor needs three separate signals to control the brightness of each colour in each set of dots. It also needs signals that make sure that the scanning starts at the top left-hand corner of the screen at exactly the time when the brightness signals for that set of dots arrive.

These timing signals are called synchronising signals, and we need one to control the scanning across the screen and another one to control the scanning down the screen. That's why the cable between the computer and the monitor is so thick — at least five signals have to be carried, and each one has to be shielded from the others so that they do not interfere with each other.

The way that the colour signals are used, and the rate of synchronising signals are both quite different from the signals used in TV sets. That's why you need an adapter to display computer pictures on a TV. You also need an adapter to show TV pictures on your monitor.

5 The drives

The drives are a very important part of your computer, and as we saw earlier, there are three types, the floppy, the hard drive and the CD-ROM drive. Of these three, the floppy drive and the hard drive can read and write data, but at present the CD-ROM drive cannot be used for writing data. That will change soon enough, because there are already drives that you can add to your PC that allow you to make compact discs filled with your own data.

These drives are important because the main memory of the computer is volatile; it loses all of its data whenever the computer is switched off. If you have created data for yourself, you will need to save it on either the hard drive or the floppy drive before you switch off. After all, if you have spent three hours typing you don't want to lose it all in one careless moment.

Most programs will remind you if you try to close them down without saving your work, but there is no way of stopping you from pressing the button that switches off the whole computer.

Floppy drive and its limitations

When small computers were first sold, data could be stored on tape, using an ordinary cassette recorder. Big computers used floppy discs, but these measured eight inches across, and were much too big to fit into a small computer. These floppy discs **were** floppy, just a thin disc of plastic inside a cardboard sleeve, looking rather the old-fashioned LP gramophone record. The plastic disc was coated with magnetic material, just like the thin tape in a sound cassette or a videocassette.

Using ordinary cassettes for recording data was never reliable, and when a smaller size of floppy disc (5¼ inch) was manufactured, a few of the small computers started to fit drives for this type of disc.

The first PC computers used a cassette recorder for storage, but they very soon changed to a 5¼ inch floppy drive. This was used for several years until the 3½ inch type of floppy disc became available. Steady progress in design and use of better materials made it possible for this small disc to hold more data that the 5¼ inch type or the 8 inch type ever could.

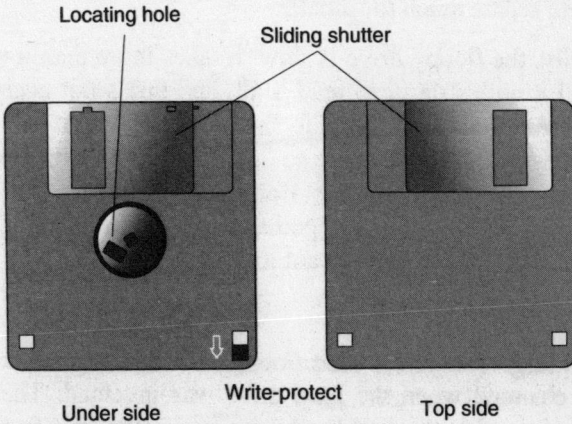

Figure 8. The 3½ inch floppy disc

In addition, the thin plastic disc that is the important part of a floppy was much better protected. Instead of a cardboard sleeve, which is easily bent, the 3½ inch disc has a rigid plastic casing which is quite remarkably tough. It's just not floppy any longer, and though we should now call it a removable disc, the old name of floppy has stuck.

Floppy discs are convenient. You can put one into the drive, read its data, or write some, and then take it out. Provided that you keep the floppy in a cool dry place, away from sunlight, it will keep the data secure for years. We don't know how long the data will keep, because floppies haven't been around for long enough, but 30 years is a good guess.

The drawback is that a floppy disc does not hold much data. The usual quantity is 1.4 Mbyte, though it's possible to squeeze up to 4 Mbyte on to one disc. At one time this would have seemed a very generous amount (particularly if you had used 8 inch floppies that held only 180 Kbyte). Nowadays we have become used to needing much more space for data and particularly for programs, and a mere 1.4 Mbyte seems much too small.

Finally, the floppy drive is slow. It takes more than a minute to fill it with data or to read it all, and that's not acceptable now. As computers become faster and faster, it would be pointless to have to wait so long for data to be read or written. We now use the floppy drive mainly for small amounts of valuable data, perhaps today's work, rather than for all the data we might want to store.

Hard drives

Even large computers used floppies at one time, but all that was changed when the hard drive was invented. The story goes about that the first hard drive was made in a factory in Winchester, USA, and certainly these drives were called Winchester discs for many years.

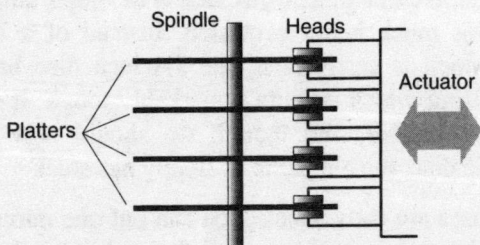

Figure 9. Platters of a hard drive

The reason for the name is simple — the disc is made from metal or other hard material, and each drive has several discs, typically 6–8 and all mounted on one shaft. Each disc is called a **platter**, and because they are hard and are enclosed in a sealed container, they can be packed with much more data on each platter. For the same reason, the shaft can be spun much faster, typically 5,600 revolutions per minute rather than the 360 used for floppies.

Speed and capacity

The end result of all this is that a hard drive can hold much more data and it can shift data (to or from the computer) much faster. The first hard drives that were fitted to small computers held 20 Mbyte, which seems a lot in the days when floppies held only 360 Kbyte, but a typical hard drive nowadays holds 1,000 Mbyte or more.

In fact, we have to use another unit for measuring their capacity. This is the Gigabyte (Gbyte), equal to 1024 Mbyte, and a modern computer usually comes with a hard drive that can be anything between 2.1 Gbyte and 6 Gbyte. The miracle of it all is that these drives are smaller and cheaper than their 20 Mbyte ancestors.

The hard drive is not (normally) removable, because the drive contains the platters and is sealed. When you switch on your computer, the program in the ROM will read from the hard drive (unless you have a floppy in its own drive). You will normally store all of your programs and all of your data on the hard drive.

This allows you to run programs faster and store your own data more quickly, but it also means all of your eggs being in one basket. Like anything mechanical, a hard drive will eventually fail. Now if a floppy drive fails, you just put in a new drive, and you lose nothing because the data is stored on the floppy discs that you keep in a safe place. If a hard drive fails, you lose all of your data because the platters are sealed inside the drive. That doesn't mean that it's totally lost, because the drive can be sent to a factory where it can be opened in a dust-free room, the platters put into another drive, and your data restored.

Restoring data like this can cost a lot of money, however, and it's better to keep your own copies of vital data. The life of a hard drive can be ten years or more, but that's no comfort if you have just switched on and nothing has happened. That's when you will be very glad that you used backup — see later.

Virtual memory

A hard drive is a way of storing data, like the memory, but with the advantage that it can contain much more data than the memory. Now that hard drives are so fast, we make use of them also as extra memory.

Now though the hard drive is fast, it's no match for the speed of the memory. We can measure the speed of reading or writing a hard drive in units of milliseconds, thousandths of a second, but memory speed is measured in nanoseconds, a million times faster.

What we can do, however, is to use the hard drive for temporary storage. Suppose you want to work with two large programs, switching between them. There might be room in memory for all of one program, and part of the other, but the rest of the second program can be held on the hard drive. When you switch programs, you might not need the portion that is on the hard drive, and even if you do, it can be read back in a short time. At the same time, part of the first program can be stored on the hard drive.

This use of a hard drive is called **virtual memory**, and it makes possible the use of several large programs together. The time needed to swap programs may be long compared to memory times, but it's still quite short compared to human timescales. After all, how fast can you type? A good typist can churn out 100 words per minute, and in the time of a few words a vast amount of data can be shifted to or from the hard drive.

The only snag is churning. If the memory is too small, data will be swapped to and from the hard drive continually, so that the drive never seems to stop. This churning is a sign that your programs are too big for your memory, and it's time you added more memory to your computer.

CD-ROM drive

The CD-ROM drive that is used at present is read-only. The disc is separate, and you can read the data on the disc, but you cannot write. This will not always be true, and perhaps by the time you read this all PC computers will be fitted with read/write CD drives.

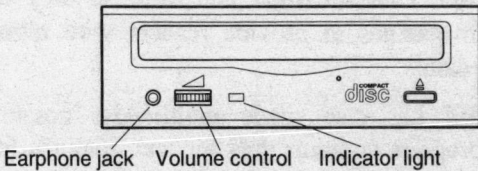

Earphone jack   Volume control   Indicator light

Figure 10. A CD-ROM drive front panel

The name, CD-ROM, reminds you that the discs you use at present are read-only, but it's likely that the name will stay the same even when the read/write drives become commonplace.

The CD-ROM drive can be used for ordinary music CDs, and if your computer contains a sound board you can play a music CD simply by inserting it into the drive. You can listen either through headphones (there is a socket and a volume control on the front panel) or through the sound-board of the computer. The important use for the CD-ROM drive, however, is for distributing programs.

At one time, programs (software) for computers were sold on floppy discs (they had been sold on tape cassettes before

41

that). You can still buy your software on floppies, but it's not very satisfactory if the program is a large one. For example, one large program might come on 32 floppies. That's a lot to work with, and the program takes a long time to install, as you feed each floppy in and out.

Of course, once you have copied the program to your hard drive, it will not need to do this work again, but you still have to find space to store all these floppy discs and keep them safe. By contrast, a CD-ROM disc will store as much as will fit on 460 floppies!

All this space allows manufacturers to add extras to programs. For example, a program to make drawings might need only 20 Mbyte of the CD, but the disc can be filled up with data files of ready-made pictures, the type we call clip-art. In addition, CDs are light and thin, so they can be attached to magazines to provide readers with masses of program and data.

The CD-ROM has also made multimedia possible. A multimedia program contains data for text, pictures (still or moving), and sounds. All of this would take up an impossible amount of space on floppies, but the CD-ROM provides all this space and more. Your CD-ROM encyclopaedia will show you text about an animal, a picture of it walking about, and the sound it makes. Educational CDs are now by far the quickest and easiest way of learning, and in the UK, the publisher Dorling Kindersley is by far the leading supplier of excellent educational CDs.

Backup drives

Backup is like insurance. If you have it and don't need it there is no harm done, but if you need it and don't have it, that's disaster.

Some day, unless you renew your computer every few years, you may have the nasty experience of a hard drive failure. You switch on, and instead of hearing the familiar whine of the hard drive motor starting, there is silence. That's when you are glad of backups, or when you wish you had made some.

It needn't be quite so dramatic. You might find that the computer starts normally, but there are programs of data that you can't get to. Notices about corrupted data appear on the screen, and your computer is crippled. That also is when you are glad that you had backups.

A backup is just another copy of a program or of your data. The habit of backing up started when floppy discs were unreliable, and it was usual to make at least three copies of all data. Things have improved since then, but the possibility of a failure is still around. What makes backup more important now is that a hard drive may contain so much data, and the thought of losing it all is not a pleasant one.

Many PC users do not bother with backup. The reliability of so much computer equipment is so good that you may never need backups. On the other hand, if you have so much to lose, why take risks?

To start with, what do you need to backup? Many programs nowadays come to you on CD-ROM, and unless you make a habit of treating CDs roughly these will still be usable for many years to come. Other programs come on floppies, and if there are not too many of them, it's reasonable to make a copy of each. That's all of your hard drive programs safe.

What is more important is your data. You might create data that was letters, accounts, articles in magazines, posters, pictures, tables of ancestors, whatever you use your computer to do. Each item must have taken you some time, and is valuable. What makes it valuable is that once you have created data you can use it over and over again. You need never type your own name and address on a letter again; you need never draw a picture or a map again if the data has been saved.

Your data, then, is the most important thing to back up. When you first start using a computer, there might be only a small amount of data that you have created, and it will all fit on one floppy. Later, you will need more floppies, but for many users this is all the backup that is needed, a few floppies kept in a safe place.

Things change if you have a large amount of data. As an example, I have the word-processor files of a hundred books with text and pictures. If you have this amount, it would take too long to put it all on to floppies, and they would take up too much space. One solution is to use a tape backup drive. These need not be expensive, some cost less than £100, and they can store much more data than a floppy (more than a CD-ROM in some cases).

Another solution is a hard drive that is removable — the casing remains in the computer, but the drive cartridge can be inserted and removed. The other development that is now available is the read-write type of CD drive, and the most recent types of drives are now reasonably priced and likely to cost even less in the near future.

6 Booting up

Booting up means switching the computer on and getting it running. As we have seen, the microprocessor inside your computer cannot start until it has code to read, and the system is arranged so that this is supplied from the ROM. Once this has been done, the computer is capable of a few actions, one of which is to read in further instructions from the hard drive or from a floppy.

If you start up with a floppy in the drive, the computer will try to read from this floppy, and you will see an error message if the floppy does not contain the codes that are expected. If you leave a floppy in the drive from your last session, you will see this message about it:

Non-system disk or disk error

If you see this error message when there is no floppy in the drive, it indicates a hard drive fault. That means big trouble ahead.

Using the ROM

The ROM of a PC machine consists usually of one chip, and it does not hold a large amount of code. There are programs called dump utilities that allow you to see what is stored inside the ROM. Though a lot of what you see means nothing unless you are a programmer, you can get some useful snippets such as the name of the manufacturer of the ROM and its code, the date, and a serial number. The data and serial number can often be important if you want to know if your ROM will be capable of some actions.

At the time when you first switch on, the computer is capable of absolutely nothing, so that the ROM is vitally important. It must supply codes, above all else, that allow the computer to read from the hard or floppy drives. There is no need to have codes for writing, or to read vast amounts of code. Once the microprocessor can read code from the drive and copy that code into memory it can really start to work. The code that it reads is called the **operating system**, and we shall come back to that point later.

In addition to being able to read the drive, the computer needs to be able to display some characters on the screen, and to respond to some keys, and there are codes in the ROM for these actions also. The keyboard is needed if you want to stop the loading of the system or if you need to make some options. This does not need all of the keyboard, only a few selected keys. For example, there will be a combination of keys that can be pressed to display the content of CMOS RAM, something we shall look at later.

A few monitor actions are needed so that you can see messages on the screen. Some of the messages are progress messages that you will see every time you boot up, telling you what stage the action has reached. Others are copyright notices, telling you who wrote the software. Others, which you hope you will not see, are error messages that tell you something has gone wrong. The message about the wrong floppy in the drive is one of these, and it will probably be the only one of quite a large number that you will ever see.

Power-on self-test

One essential part of the ROM codes is the self-testing code that carries out checks on the computer. These are not detailed checks, which would take too long, but rough checks that would indicate if there were a serious fault. The drives are checked, as you would expect, and so is the memory, and you will, on many machines, receive a progress report that shows the memory has passed its test for reading and writing.

Exactly what is done depends on who wrote the code in the ROM, and different manufacturers provide different codes. The important thing is to get used to what appears, so that you will know if something unusual has happened. This might indicate a real problem, or it might be the machine's response to a change that you have made, like fitting more memory or adding another hard drive.

CMOS RAM

The ROM can't do everything that is needed at the time when you switch on. In particular, there is some vital information that it doesn't hold, such as the size of the memory and the type of hard drive. That type of information **could**, of course, be held on the ROM, but what would you do if you wanted to add more memory or use a different hard drive, or add another drive? If the information were held in the ROM, you would need to change the ROM.

This was not a worry in the early days of the PC machine, because there was no hard drive, and the machine came with as much memory as could be fitted. Nowadays, things are different, and you need to be able to add memory and drives as the software becomes more bulky (and slower to run).

The solution is a type of memory we have not mentioned so far, called CMOS RAM. It is memory that can be read and written, but it is constructed in a way (that's the CMOS part) that allows it to retain information if a low-voltage battery is connected. The current that the CMOS RAM takes from this battery is so small that the battery will usually last for the lifetime of the computer. Some machines have connectors inside the case for ordinary batteries, but most use the built-in battery exclusively.

So what do we keep in the CMOS RAM? To start with, it holds information on the drives. It notes whether there is one floppy or two (a bit out of date now) and, more important, it keeps a note of information on the hard drive, with provision for a second hard drive if needed. This information is essential if the computer is to be able to read the drives, and the type of information is typically the number of platters, and how the drive is divided into units called tracks and sectors.

Unlike a floppy, there is no standard form of hard drive. You need to be able to read floppies that have been made on other machines. You do not expect to take the platters out of a hard drive and put them into another one, so there is no point in having a standard system for hard drives. Removable hard drives keep the platters in a sealed container and are intended to be used only with the outer unit that belong with the cartridge.

Another action that the CMOS RAM carries out is to keep the date and time information. The same battery that keeps the CMOS RAM from losing data also supplies a quartz clock circuit, called a real-time clock. This way, your computer retains date and time data even when it is switched off. Old PCs did not, and you had to type in the date and time at every boot. If your PC suddenly needs to know the time, something is wrong, and it's usually the battery for the CMOS RAM.

You very seldom need to know what is stored in the CMOS RAM, and you seldom see the screen display that appears when the settings have to be changed. There are two events that can display this (all provided for by codes in the ROM). One is a change, such as adding memory or a new hard drive. The other is pressing some keys at the time when you are booting up.

What keys? I can't tell you, because it varies from one type of ROM chip to another. A typical combination is Ctrl–Alt–S, meaning that you press these three keys together, but you might find that you needed Ctrl–Alt–Esc or some other combination. The Ctrl and Alt keys are usually needed along with another key.

When you use these keys at boot time, or if the action is triggered by a change that you have made, you will see the CMOS RAM screen appear. You can then alter the values that appear — but you have to obey the instructions on the screen because you may only be able to use a limited range of keys.

Date (day/date/year): Wed, 25 June 1997					Base Memory : 640 KB		
Time (hour/min/sec) : 10 : 47 : 12					Ext. memory 31744 KB		
Daylight saving : Disabled	Cyln	Head	WPcom	LZone	Sect	Size	
Hard Disk C: type : 47 = USER TYPE	622	128	0	4981	63	2568 MB	
Hard Disk D: type : Not Installed							
Floppy drive A: : 1.44 MB, 3½"							
Floppy drive B: : Not installed	Sun	Mon	Tue	Wed	Thu	Fri	Sat
Primary Display : EGA/VGA/	1	2	3	4	5	6	7
Keyboard : Installed	8	9	10	11	12	13	14
	15	16	17	18	19	20	21
Month : Jan, Feb,...Dec	22	23	24	25	26	27	28
Date : 01, 02, 03,......31	29	30	1	2	3	4	5
Year : 1981, 1982,...2099							
ESC: Exit Arrow keys: Select F2/F3 : Color PU/PD : Modify							

Figure 11. A CMOS RAM display

This shows the essential information on drives and memory, along with date and time settings, and you should note down the figures that appear for the hard drive. If anything should happen that wipes the CMOS RAM memory, you must be able to supply these figures again.

Why? Because without these the hard drive cannot be read correctly. You might, of course, be able to make a guess and get it working in a crippled way, but that's not good enough. If you have a note of the figures, or use one of the little utility programs that saves the CMOS RAM settings on a floppy disc, then loss of the CMOS RAM data is not so much of a threat.

Why should it fail? The most obvious (and most frequent) cause is that the battery has packed up. These batteries normally have a long life, but there's always the exception, and it might, as they say, be **you**. If the battery fails, it can be replaced, but this does not replace the information, so you will be glad that you saved it in some form or another.

The operating system

The final booting action of the code in the ROM is to read more code from the hard drive. This does not mean that the code in the ROM is not needed again. In fact some of the code in the ROM is used continually, because it controls the most important actions like using disc drives. That, however, is not really enough, because you expect a computer to be able to do a lot more than just read and write from and to drives.

There was a time when each program that you bought (or wrote!) had to contain code for all the ordinary everyday actions such as controlling the keyboard, monitor, drives, use of memory and so on. As computers developed, however, we found that it made more sense to have a single program that dealt with all these tasks, called 'housekeeping', so that other programs could make use of the codes. The housekeeping program is called the operating system, and the older name was DOS, meaning disc operating system, because the use of discs was the main reason for having an operating system.

Nowadays this is firmly established. A program performs actions by using some code of its own, and also making use of code in the operating system for actions that are housekeeping actions. Some of the codes in the operating system may use codes in the ROM, so that you can think of three layers of codes being used in this way. The ROM codes serve the simplest and most common actions and the operating system provides other important actions such as copying data from one disc to another or operating a printer.

Operating systems have grown over the years to provide much more than the basic needs of a computer. They now provide for actions such as control of sound, using CD-ROM, organising data into groups called folders and much more.

7 Running programs

Now here is what you bought a computer for — to run programs (often called applications). The reason for using a PC machine is that it can run programs of any kind. You might like games, working on accounts, drawing pictures, looking up information in an encyclopædia, listening to music, editing film, making contacts over the Internet. All these actions can be done with the same PC. In computer-speak, you use the same **hardware** with different **software**.

In Chapter 6 we looked at the way that the PC is controlled as being like a layer cake, with the application controlling the operating system and the operating system using the ROM. Now we can look at what is involved, and at a few more layers.

Filenames

First of all, we have to look at names. Your hard drive will contain programs and it will contain data that you have created. Each item is a **file**, a collection of codes. The program files contain codes that are instructions for the microprocessor. Your data files contain ASCII codes for letters and numbers, codes for shapes and colours, codes for sounds; whatever type of files you create with the program that you use.

These file need to be identified. You cannot type a command that reads: *use the writing program to look at the letter I wrote yesterday*. So far, computers do not understand language like that, called *natural language*. Instead, you have to use commands, and these commands make use of a name for each file, its **filename**.

Programs have file names that belong to them, and you must use the correct name to run the file. If your typing program is called SCRIBE then that's the name you have to use, you cannot use any other name, and you must spell SCRIBE absolutely perfectly each time you want to use it.

You have more freedom with the files that you create, because you can select a name for yourself. The freedom is limited, though, because if you use the DOS operating system you must keep the name limited to a maximum of 8 characters that are letters or digits (no points, colons, commas or other marks allowed). Longer names are allowed if you use Windows 95 or later versions.

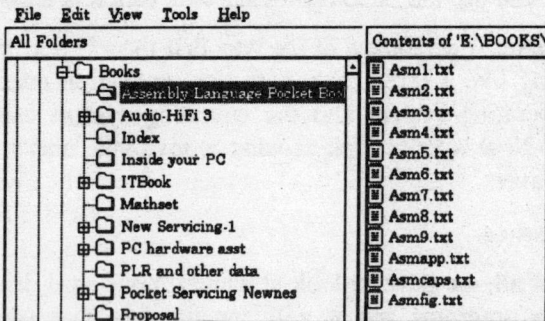

Figure 12. A files list displayed by Windows 95

One exception is that you are allowed to use an extension to a name. This extension can consist of up to three letters or digits, and is separated from the main name by a full-stop. For example, you might have a file that was of a letter, and you could call it TOJIM or TOJIM.DOC or TOJAMES.TXT. Using extensions for your files is a useful way to identify the type of file (text, accounts, drawings, whatever).

Program files can also use extensions, and the letters that are used are COM or EXE. The difference is not important; the COM file is usually a much smaller file than the EXE type.

What is important is not confusing the files. You can use a word processor program to read and display a file called

THISTEXT.DOC, but not a file that is called THISTEXT.EXE. The DOC file will consist mainly of ASCII codes that display as characters on the screen. The EXE file contains codes for actions, and what you see on the screen makes no sense.

Running DOS

From the first, the PC machine was designed to use an operating system. This system was written for the PC by Microsoft Inc. for IBM, and it was called PC-DOS. An identical operating system was also sold to other users and called MS-DOS. This DOS has always been the main operating system for the PC.

When DOS is loaded from the hard drive it indicates when it is ready for a command by showing the identification letter for the drive. Since the hard drive is always the C drive, the screen shows C:\ when DOS is ready. If you had loaded in DOS from a floppy, the signal would be A:\.

You can then command DOS to do what you want. It's not quite so easy as that, though. First of all, you have to type the command, and you signal that the command is complete by pressing the key that we call RETURN or ENTER, usually the key that is marked by the arrow sign ◄┘

The commands of DOS are simple words, and only a limited number (a hundred or so) are recognised, words such as COPY, MOVE, TYPE and so on. A few commands need only the command word, but most others need one or more additional bits of information, called an *argument*. For example, if you wanted to copy all that was contained on a disc in the A: (floppy) drive to the C: (hard) drive, you would type:

COPY A:*.* C: (the spaces are important)

— all that follows the word COPY is the argument for this command. The argument is the way of saying exactly what it is that you want the command to work on. In this example, the argument shows that you want to copy everything in the A: drive to the C: drive.

To use DOS, then, you have to know what command words you can use, and what arguments have to follow each word. You type your command and arguments, press the RETURN key, and the action is carried out at bewildering speed. You know when the machine is ready for another command because you will see the C:\ sign appear again.

Things like copying are all very well, and very useful, but how do you run a program? A program file, remember, will be one that has the extension letters COM or EXE. You can command the computer to run the program simply by typing its main name, ignoring the COM or EXE part. For example if you have a program called TVPROG.COM on a floppy in the A: drive, you can type the command:

A:\TVPROG

— to run this program. If you have a program called FRIENDS.EXE on the C: drive, you can use the command:

C:\FRIENDS

— to run this program.

Using data files does not depend on DOS commands. If you have a file that was created by a program called SCRIBE, for example, you must run the SCRIBE program to read the data file. How the reading action is done then depends on the program, it need not be anything like a DOS command. You might, for example, see on the screen a menu of files that are available and select one.

Running Windows

Operating systems such as DOS had been used for many years before the Xerox laboratories in California dreamt up a very different way of using the computer. The idea was that files, commands, and actions would be represented by pictures that could be moved around the screen. The movement was controlled by a small trolley that was called a **mouse** that controlled the position of a pointer on the screen.

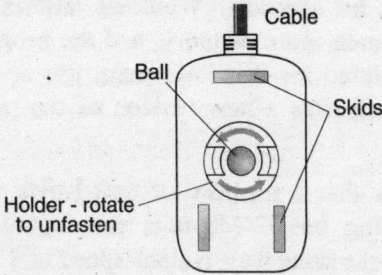

Figure 13. A mouse seen from underneath

To delete a file, for example, you moved the pointer over the image or **icon** that represented the file, pressed a button on the mouse, and then moved the mouse, this time with the icon attached to the pointer, to drop the icon into a dustbin icon. To run a program, you put the pointer over the filename and image and clicked a button twice.

This type of action was called **WIMP**, meaning Window, Icon, Mouse, Pointer, in the beginning, and renamed **GUI** (graphics user interface) later. The idea that emerged at Xerox was taken up first by Apple computers, and has now developed into Windows for the PC.

Windows has been strengthened and refined over the years, and the version that has made most impact is Windows 95. The principles are the same, however, using the mouse to move the pointer, to drag icons around, and to click twice to run a program.

When Windows is used, the machine boots, loads DOS, and then loads Windows. This takes longer, and because Windows uses the DOS commands, it adds another layer to the cake. You select what you want to do, Windows issues the DOS commands, and DOS makes use of ROM and other codes to carry out the actions.

Because Windows is another layer of command, it needs a faster computer than you would need if you simply used DOS programs. In addition, Windows allows the PC machine to use much more memory, and the programs that are now being written for Windows make use of more and more memory each time a new version of the program is written.

We used to think that a memory of 640 Kbyte was good enough for anything, but 32 Mbyte is now regarded as just about average. In the same way, a clock speed of 8 MHz was good enough for DOS programs; we are now looking at 200 MHz and more to get programs to run at a reasonable speed.

Programming for DOS and Windows

The early days of computers were the fun times, because we learned so much for ourselves by writing programs for the machines. We had to write our own programs because there was no other way of using the machines, and it could be very tedious if we wanted to do anything complicated.

Nowadays, you do not need to write programs, because there is a such an enormous variety of software already written and waiting to be used. If you use DOS, the choice is bewildering and most of the programs that are available are either free or cost very little. If you use Windows, there is a large choice, though most programs are more expensive — but remember that if you use Windows your PC can be used in DOS as well, because Windows is an addition to DOS.

If you want to learn to program, then it's easier to program for DOS and a programming program (if you see what I mean) is included with MS-DOS. It's called QBASIC, and it is a variety of a well-established programming language called BASIC that was used on almost all of the small computers in the past.

Programming for Windows can be done using a language called Visual Basic. This, however, is expensive, and though it can create splendid programs, it is not easy to learn.

8 Odds and ends

In this quick tour of discovery inside your PC we have inevitably missed out some items. That's not because they were unimportant, more usually it's because to explain them at the time would have meant adding too much detail. Now is the time and place to add these items, particularly now that you have a much better idea of what goes on inside your computer. We start with a little more about something that is not part of the computer, the monitor.

Resolution and colours

The monitor displays the output of your computer, and it's a vital part of the equipment. In the old days, a monitor showed only black and white text, not pictures, and the quality was no better than that of a TV receiver. Nowadays we expect much more, and we measure how much more we get in terms of resolution and number of colours.

The resolution of a monitor means how many separate coloured dots we could see across the screen width and down the screen depth. The 'ordinary' resolution is 640 × 480, meaning 640 dots across and 480 down. The reason that we have fewer dots in the down direction is that the screen is not square, it is wider than it is deep. The ratio of width to depth is 4:3, just as for TV, and the 640 × 480 resolution means about 75 dots per inch. Compare this to a printer that can easily achieve 300 dots per inch.

♦ Incidentally, a TV receiver is hard pressed to get a resolution of around 400 × 310.

As the PC developed, programs were being written for creating very precise drawings, and monitors capable of higher resolution, such as 800 × 600 or 1024 × 768, started to appear. These needed software drivers (see later) to make use of the higher resolution. Nowadays, most monitors are capable of at least 800 × 600 resolution.

Another point that affects the monitor is the number of bits that the PC computer uses to code colour. In the beginning, it took only one bit — 0 for black and 1 for white. We moved on to use four bits, which allowed 16 colours to be displayed. This does not mean that only sixteen colours can ever be displayed, but that any one picture cannot use more than sixteen. You could create a picture with one set of sixteen colours, and another picture with a different set, so long as no picture contain more than sixteen.

The next step was to use eight bits, a complete byte, for colour coding. This allows a picture to contain up to 256 colours, and this is the minimum number that is acceptable for pictures in multimedia programs.

Inevitably, the next step was to use two bytes, with 16 bits coding up to 64,000 colours (approximately). Though the difference between a 16-colour picture and a 256-colour picture is obvious, the difference between 256 and 64,000 is not quite so clear. If, however, you are trying to reproduce a colour photograph on the screen, there is definitely a difference.

The next step was to use 24 bits, giving a maximum, in theory, of around 16 million possible colours. This colour setting is often called 'photo real' because it allows the screen to reproduce colour photographs perfectly.

What does it all mean for your computer? The answer is speed and memory. The higher the resolution that you use, the more screen dots need to be controlled. This needs more space in the memory, and takes longer to process. Similarly, if 24 bits are used for each set of colour dots, you need much more memory than for 4 bits, and the processing of the image takes much longer.

What it all amounts to is that you should use the resolution and colour numbers that suit your software. If you **must** work with images of the quality of a photograph, then use high resolution and 24-bit colour by all means. You will have to use a **very** fast machine with a lot of memory and a huge hard drive — each picture might need up to 32 Mbyte of hard drive space!

If you are using your computers for word processing, accounts, line drawings, route planing; all the 'ordinary' type of actions, you don't need high resolution or a lot of colours. Using 640 × 480 resolution and 4-bit (16 colour) settings will allow you to use a slower machine with less memory, or work faster with the computer you have.

Direct memory access

Direct memory access (DMA) is a system that grew up along with the PC machine. A large part of what a computer does makes use of data bytes being copied into or out of the memory. On older designs, this was done using the microprocessor to read each byte and copy it wherever it was supposed to go. The effect, of course, is that the microprocessor cannot do anything else while the copying is going on.

DMA works by using a separate chip for this copying action. The microprocessor must still be used, but all it does is to program the DMA chip with the location of the bytes, the number to be copied, and the destination. Once that has been done in a few clock ticks, the DMA chip does the rest, so that the microprocessor is free to get on with what it is paid to do.

The chipset

Though the microprocessor is the kingpin chip inside your PC, the chips that are used to support it are also important — this collection is referred to as the chipset. Modern fast microprocessors would be crippled if they did not have a set of chips to back them up, such as the DMA chip we have just referred to.

The chipset on the motherboard is therefore important, and when you upgrade a computer by fitting a new motherboard and processor you have to be certain that the motherboard is one that will assist the processor to work as fast and efficiently as possible.

These chipsets are being refined and improved as quickly as are the processor chips. If you are buying another computer or upgrading the present one by replacing the motherboard, you have to keep an eye on what is the most recent chipset.

♦   This means that there will be a lot of shops and mail-order firms selling the older chipsets so as to get rid of them before everyone knows about the new ones.

Drivers

A driver is not a chip, it's a piece of software, and it's intended to allow your computer to make use of another item of hardware.

Your computer almost certainly uses a mouse, and plugging a mouse into a socket at the back of the computer doesn't make the mouse useful — after all, plugging in a light bulb has no effect unless you also switch the light on. What is needed is software code that allows the computer to use the mouse, and that's the driver.

The printer is another item that needs a driver. At one time, it was enough to send ASCII codes to a printer, but since printers have improved as fast as computers we expect to be able to print in fancy styles, print pictures, avoid printing some codes and so on. Each make of printer is likely to use different codes for effects like bold type, italic type, printing pictures in dots and so on.

This needs a driver, and at one time all software came with a set of drivers for all the popular printers. Nowadays, the use of Windows is so common that a printer needs just one driver for Windows. The software that uses Windows will use the Windows driver with no need for a separate one. If you use DOS, your software will have to include a driver for each popular make of printer.

♦ Programs that run using DOS alone will not be able to make use of Windows drivers.

Drivers can cause a problem if you buy a new printer. If the printer was being made at the time when you installed Windows it's likely that Windows has a suitable driver available. If the printer is a very new model, there will be no driver in your version of Windows, and you may be able to use another driver (for a similar model from the same manufacturer). Another possibility is that the printer will come with a disc of drivers that includes one suitable for Windows.

Monitors also need drivers, and here again Windows scores because once you have a good Windows driver installed, all of your Windows software can use it. There are not nearly so many variations of monitors as there are of printers, but you need a good selection of drivers to cope with different resolutions and number of colours.

Drivers can cause problems. Some are poorly designed, and monitor drivers are often the cause of problems. Windows users should try the Microsoft drivers rather than drivers supplied with a monitor. Beware of bargain offers of monitors that have no driver for Windows available.

Address and interrupt numbers

With luck, you won't need to know this, but we aren't always lucky (it might never be you). Every device (printer, mouse, monitor and so on) that is connected to the computer needs to have a code number, an address, that the microprocessor can use to identify it. Even some chips, like the DMA chip, need this type of identification.

At one time, not so very long ago, if you added anything to your computer system you had to make sure that it was using an address number that was free and not used by anything else. If two devices use the same address, the computer cannot be expected to sort it all out, and the result is a conflict — something will stop working.

The same applies to interrupts. We have seen already how the keyboard can create an interrupt to ensure that the microprocessor will attend to it. A lot of other devices and chips also use interrupt signals, and once again these are identified by code numbers, the interrupt numbers. The trouble here is that the PC machine was designed with a rather small number of interrupt numbers available.

This makes conflicts more likely; as it can often be difficult to ensure that a new device will not use the same interrupt number as another one. It's not always a disaster, because sometimes two devices are never used at the same time, so that sharing is perfectly possible. You can't be sure, though, and this is another setting that you had to attend to at one time.

Nowadays, if you use Windows 95 (or later versions), you have the benefit of what is called Plug'n'Play. This is a way of avoiding conflicts, and it uses a combination of some codes contained in a ROM inside each device, and codes in Windows used to check these ROMs. If you buy a device that is certified as Plug'n'Play, you can do just that: plug it into a socket, switch the computer on, and make use of the new device. Only someone who has experienced the task of installing new equipment before Plug'n'Play can know just how much work this avoids!

Appendices

A

Hexadecimal numbers

All computing, as we have seen, depends on the use of number codes. Each of these numbers is stored as a set of 1s and 0s. Binary code like this is fine for machines, because with only two possibilities to work with, the chances of the machine making a mistake become very remote. Humans, however, are not ideally suited to working in binary numbers without making mistakes, simply because the stream of 1s and 0s becomes confusing, and an obvious step is to use a more convenient number scale.

Just what is a more convenient number scale is quite another matter. Most people work with the ordinary 0 to 9 scale of numbers based on counting in tens (denary numbers). Memory analysing programs like MSD, and memory management programs of all types, however, are written as much for the convenience of professional programmers, who use hexadecimal numbers, as for the ordinary computer user. Hexadecimal means scale of sixteen, and the reason that it is used so extensively is that it is naturally suited to representing binary bytes.

Four bits, half of a byte, will represent numbers which lie in the range 0 to 15 in our ordinary number scale. This is the range of one hex digit. Since we don't have symbols for digits higher than 9, we have to use the letters A, B, C, D, E, and F to supplement the digits 0 to 9 in the hex scale. The advantage is that a byte of data can be represented by a two digit number and a complete address by a five digit number.

The table, following, shows the hex and binary equivalents of numbers 1 to 15 in denary.

Binary	Denary	Hex	Binary	Denary	Hex
00	0	00	1000	8	08
01	1	01	1001	9	09
10	2	02	1010	10	0A
11	3	03	1011	11	0B
100	4	04	1100	12	0C
101	5	05	1101	13	0D
110	6	06	1110	14	0E
111	7	07	1111	15	0F

The maximum size of a single byte, 255 in denary, is FF in hex, and this hex number is $15 \times 16 + 15$.

When we write hex numbers, it's usual to mark them in some way so that you don't confuse them with denary numbers. There's not much chance of confusing a number like 3E with a denary number, but a number like 26 might be hex or denary. The convention that is followed by many programmers is to use a capital H to mark a hex number, with the H sign placed after the number. Most of the MS-DOS memory utilities assume that you will type in hex numbers, and they will not work with anything else, and addresses in MSD make use of hex numbers also.

B

Using disc and memory readers

This is advanced stuff, but you should know that it's possible. Normally, you make use of discs and memory by using your normal software. This is fine when all is well, but when there is a disc fault you usually cannot get your software to read or write the disc.

You can, however, buy software that lets you see on screen what codes are stored on the disc or in the memory. This is real power over the machine, and it has to be used with care. This type of software will usually allow you to alter the codes as well as read them, and you can do a lot of damage if you alter codes without knowing what you are doing.

Software of this type is often referred to as Tools or Utilities, and famous names are Norton Utilities and PC Tools. If this aspect of using your PC sounds interesting, giving you the ability to read floppy discs that were not created by a PC machine, or to find a fault in a hard drive, then have a go — but you need to be careful. One golden rule is that you must always have backups of any data on a hard drive. Another is that you must never change anything on the hard drive unless you are absolutely sure that is will not make the drive unusable. If you do totally corrupt a hard drive, the only thing that is left is to reformat it and reinstall all the software. If you use Windows, this is a difficult task and one that needs a lot of knowledge and experience. Be warned.

♦ If, however, you want to get some experience of reading codes without the hazards of writing them, DOS contains a utility called MSD that you can use, and it can be used even if you normally work with Windows.

C

Choosing hardware

If you want to add hardware to your computer, such as a new internal board (like a video display card) or some external device (such as a scanner), make quite certain that the board or device will match your computer. If you use Windows 95 (or later version) make it clear to the shop that you want equipment that is compatible, meaning Plug'n'Play.

The same applies to items like adding memory or another hard drive. Don't assume that everything will work with your computer. Memory boards come in several varieties, and some will quite certainly not be suitable. Similarly hard drives come in two main varieties (IDE and SCSI) and only one type will be suitable. In addition, if your computer is an older type it may not be able to use large hard drives (more than 512 Mbyte).

D

Some common abbreviations

This is not by any means a complete list, but it contains most of the common abbreviations that you will find applied in computing.

ANSI American National Standards Institute, used for a number code system that follows the ASCII set for numbers 32 to 127, and specifies characters for the set 128 to 255.

ASCII American Standard Code for Information Interchange, the number code for letters, numerals and punctuation marks that uses the numbers 32 to 127. Text files are normally ASCII or ANSI coded.

AT Advanced Technology, letters used by IBM in 1982 for the computer that succeeded the PC/XT.

BIOS Basic Input Output System, the program in a ROM chip that allows the computer to make use of screen, disc and keyboard, and which can used by the operating system.

CAD Computer Aided Design, a program that allows the computer to produce technical drawings to scale.

CD-ROM A form of read-only memory, consisting of a compact disc whose digital information can be read as a set of files.

CGA Colour Graphics Adapter, an early type of video graphics card.

CISC Complex Instruction Set Chip, a microprocessor which can act on any of a very large number (typically more than 300) instructions. All of the Intel microprocessors to date are of this type. See also RISC.

CMOS Complementary Metal-Oxide Semiconductor, a form of chip construction that requires a very low current.

As applied to memory, a chip that allows its contents to be retained by applying a low voltage at negligible current.

CP/M Control, Program, Monitor, one of the first standard operating systems for small computers.

CPU Central Processing Unit, the main microprocessor chip of a computer.

CRT Cathode Ray Tube, the display device for monitors used with desktop machines.

CTS Clear To Send, a coded signal used in the serial RS-232 system.

DCE Data Communications Equipment, a device such as a computer that send out serial data along a line.

DIL Dual In Line, a pin arrangement for chips that uses two lines of parallel pins.

DIP Dual in Line Package, a set of miniature switches arranged in the same form of package as a DIL chip.

DOS Disc Operating System, the programs that provides the commands that make a computer usable.

DSR Data Set Ready, a coded signal used in the serial RS-232 system.

DTE Data Terminal Equipment, a receiver of serial data such as a modem.

DTR Data Terminal Ready, a coded signal used in the serial RS-232 system.

DTP Desktop Publishing, the use of a computer for composing type and graphics into book or newspaper pages.

EEMS Enhanced Expanded Memory System, a standard for adding memory to PC/XT machines, not used on modern machines.

EGA Enhanced Graphics Adapter, another early graphic card type.

EISA Enhanced Industry Standard Architecture, a system for connecting chips in a PC machine which allows faster signal interchange than the standard (ISA) method that has been used since the early PC/AT models.

EMS Expanded Memory System, the original standard for adding memory to the PC/XT machine running DOS, now seldom used.

GEM Graphics Environmental Manager, an early GUI program.

JPEG Joint Picture Expert Group, a standard system for coding pictures into very small files.

LCD Liquid Crystal Display, a form of shadow display which is used on calculators and portable computers. It depends on the action of materials to polarise light when an electrical voltage is applied.

LCS Liquid Crystal Shutter, an array of LCD elements used to control light and so expose the light-sensitive drum in a laser printer. The LCD bar is used as an alternative to the use of a laser beam.

LED Light Emitting Diode, a device used for warning lights, and also as a form of light source in laser-style printers.

MCA Micro Channel Architecture, a bus system that was intended to replace the AT-bus (ISA). Not now used.

MDA Monochrome Display Adapter, the first type of video card used in IBM PC machines.

MIDI Musical Instrument Digital Interface, a standard form of serial data code used to allow electronic instruments to be controlled by a computer, or to link them with each other.

MMX Multi-media Extended, a form of Pentium chip that can deal faster with multimedia files.

MPEG Motion Picture Expert Group, a standard for files of moving pictures in digital form.

MS-DOS Microsoft Disk Operating System, the standard operating system for the PC type of machine.

NTSC National Television Standards Committee, the body that drew up the specification for the colour TV system used in the USA and Japan since 1952.

OCR Optical Character Recognition, software that can be used on a scanned image file to convert images of characters into ASCII codes.

OS/2 An operating system devised by IBM and intended to replace PC-DOS (the IBM version of MS-DOS).

PAL Phase Alternating Line, the colour TV system devised by Telefunken in Germany and used throughout Europe apart from France.

PBX Private Branch Exchange, sometimes a problem for using modems.

PSS Packet Switch Stream, a method of transmitting digital signals efficiently along telephone lines.

RAM Random Access Memory. All memory is random-access, but this acronym is used to mean read-write as distinct from read-only memory.

RGB Red Green Blue, the three primary colour signals. A monitor described as RGB needs to be supplied with three separate colour signals, unlike a TV monitor that can use a composite signal.

RISC Reduced Instruction Set Chip. A microprocessor that can work with only a few simple instructions, each of which can be completed very rapidly.

RLL Run Length Limited, a form of high-density recording for hard discs.

ROM Read-Only Memory, the form of non-volatile memory that is not erased when the power is switched off.

RS-232   The old standard for serial communications.

RTS Request to Send, a coded signal used in the serial RS-232 system.

SCART   The standard form of connector for video equipment, used on TV receivers and video recorders.

SCSI Small Computer Systems Interface, a form of fast-acting disc drive interface which allows for almost unlimited expansion.

SECAM   Sequence Colour et Mémoire, the French colour TV system, also used in Eastern Europe and the countries of the former USSR.

SIMM   Single Inline Memory Module, a slim card carrying memory chips, used for inserting memory in units of several Mbytes.

TIFF Tagged Image File Format, one method of coding graphics images that is widely used by scanners.

TSR Terminate and Stray Resident, a form of DOS program that runs and remains in the memory to influence the computer.

VDU Visual Display Unit, another name for the monitor.

VEGA   Video Extended Graphics Association, a group of US manufacturers who have agreed on a common standard for high-resolution graphics cards

VGA Video Graphics Array, the video card introduced by IBM for their PS/2 range of computers.

INDEX

Inside your PC

Inside your PC

NOTES

NOTES